The Glass Bottom Boat

written by Kelly Gaffney,
illustrated by Cherie Zamazing

"Mum," said Milly as they walked along the jetty.
"Look at that funny orange boat with glass on the bottom."

"Yes," said Mum
as she turned to Milly.
"That boat is called
a glass bottom boat."

GLASS BOTTO
BOAT RIDES

GLASS BOTTOM BOAT

"Can we go out
in the glass bottom boat today?"
asked Milly.
"There are no big waves
in the blue sea."

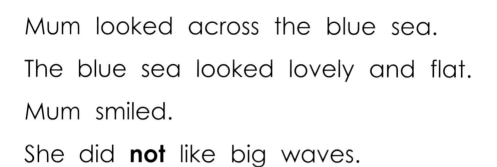

Mum looked across the blue sea.

The blue sea looked lovely and flat.

Mum smiled.

She did **not** like big waves.

"Yes!" said Mum.

"We **can** go out

in the glass bottom boat today.

Let's go and buy two tickets."

GLASS BOTTOM
BOAT RIDES

Milly and Mum went over
to the people selling tickets.
They got two tickets,
then they got
into the glass bottom boat.

Milly and Mum sat and looked into the glass at the bottom of the boat.

"Oh, look!" cried Milly.

"I can see five tiny yellow fish under the boat.

They are swimming around under the glass."

"Yes, I can see them, too," smiled Mum.

"And I can see a blue starfish. It's right under us!"

The boat took off slowly from the jetty.
It went a very long way out into the blue sea.

13

"Look at the little green fish
under the boat," said Mum.
"They are trying to hide
in the red coral."

"Yes," said Milly.
"They are hiding
from the big red fish."
Milly and Mum were out
in the boat for a long time.

When the boat came back
to the jetty,
Milly looked up at Mum.
"Thank you, Mum," she smiled.
"That was lots of fun!"